You can walk the golden road of success...

Acknowledgments

My grateful thanks go to Greg Yolen for his superb designing, Rose Tarlow who gave me the first tools to 'Do It', Adam Brand who has been a constant source of inspiration and support, Ken Davis who helped me take a huge step, and to all those who generously donated their success stories to make up this book.

To Shiela Dansinger
whose immense generosity
can do anything

Touchstone Publications
518 19th Ave., N. E., Minneapolis, Mn., 55418, USA
WWW.You-Have-What-It-Takes.com
E-Mail: Julia @ You-Have-What-It-Takes.com
Tel: 1- 800 - 580 - 2512

First published in The United States in 1998
Copyright © Julia Hastings, 1997
ISBN 0 952 0282 71

Cover by Greg Yolen,
Cartoons, book design and typesetting by Julia Hastings
Printing by MGB Printing Services Inc., Mpls., MN

How We Did It

Ordinary People Who Have Done Extraordinary Things Through

Mental Picturing

By Julia Hastings

Born in California, Julia Hastings is a psychologist who specialises in coaching the art of mental picturing. She works with many multi-national companies, appears on television and radio, gives talks and leads regular seminars. For more information write to:

Touchstone Publications
518 19th Ave., N. E.,
Minneapolis, Mn., 55418, USA

WWW.You-Have-What-It-Takes.com
E-Mail:
Julia @ You-Have-What-It-Takes.com
Tel: 1- 800 - 580 - 2512

CONTENTS

Chapter 1   An Ancient Skill.................................. 5

Chapter 2   David Made A Million....................... 7

Chapter 3   Bob's Wolverines...............................13

Chapter 4   Chris Conquered Cancer 15

Chapter 5   Charting Your Future........................23

Chapter 6   Susie Harris' Golden Road 25

Chapter 7   Mind Bending....................................31

Chapter 8   Christina Found Her Man.................33

Chapter 9   Mental Movies 41

Chapter 10   Mike Saved The Show.......................43

Chapter 11   Reverse Disaster 49

Chapter 12   Greg Healed Broken Arms 51

Chapter 13   Kids Today Are Scared 57

Chapter 14   Rick Got It Together.........................59

Chapter 15   Famous Greeks...................................63

Chapter 16   Lynn's Career Breakthrough 65

Chapter 17   Your Golden Road 71

Chapter 18   Making It Happen 73

               Contacting Julia Hastings 78

All the stories in this book are true. The people who donated their stories can be contacted directly through their addresses listed on page 78. Chris Banks is a composite character who represents common facets of countless people who have overcome life-threatening illness through using mental picturing.

Cave dwellers in the Ice Age used mental picturing...

Chapter One

An Ancient Skill

Mental picturing is the art of deliberate daydreaming. All winners use it.

It is an ancient skill. In the Ice Age, cave dwellers in France, Spain and Africa used mental picturing to insure a successful hunt. They painted pictures of animals they wanted to hunt on the walls of their caves. They then gathered around a huge roaring fire and stared at those animals until they became absolutely *real* to them.

Then they broke into a dance where they speared the animals. Spearing them was a way of actually mental picturing *in advance* a *hugely successful hunt*. Spear marks were clearly visible to anthropologists who studied their caves 80,000 years later. Cave dwellers used mental picturing in 60,000-10,000 B.C.

You may be on your own hunt. You may be hunting for a job, a partner, passing marks on your exams, better health or a fortune. The next chapter shows how 'slow learner' David Reecher used mental picturing the way the cave dwellers did to make a million.

I wasn't a slow learner, I was a big dreamer...

Chapter Two

David Made A Million

Thirty-seven year old David Reecher is president of his own brian-child, the multi-million dollar Great Wisdom Publishing, Inc. In one year David has grown his company by 300%. His energy and enthusiasm are fascinating. "I had this driving need to prove all those saps wrong." says David.

A Slow Learner

"I was classified as a slow learner in school and was sent to special classes. I wasn't really a slow learner, I was just a big dreamer. I found school work boring and became lazy. I went along with the teachers and attended their special classes. They were so easy it gave me plenty of extra time to day dream.

"My teacher told my mother, 'He's not going to set the world on fire.' But I knew someday I would. I wanted to be an exceptional businessman and run a large, influential company. And I wanted to build it with own hands. The way I built it was to picture it first in my imagination.

I Had 'Made It'

"I didn't know exactly what I wanted to do, but I knew two things: I was going to improve peoples lives and make a fortune. Even though I didn't know the details of my career, I could picture exactly what my life would be once I had 'made it'. I *saw* myself being interviewed on Good Morning America I imagined Barbara Walters coming to my private ranch to interview me. I *heard* myself saying things that impressed them. I was America's Child — an American Dream come true. I pictured these scenes over and over.

Fast Track

"Picturing how life would be once I'd made it helped me see how to fast-track my career. The more I pictured the more hungry for success and recognition I became. I had barely scraped through high school because I got into so much trouble, but I persuaded a college to accept me on probation. I studied aviation and got good marks. Then I landed a job as a junior mechanic with Presidential Airways. Within five years I moved jobs a couple of times and ended up running the entire powerplant programme for Aerotest Airlines.

"I kept picturing this fantastic future for myself, being interviewed, wealthy and well-respected. The result was that I developed an overwhelming desire to save money. If I was to create something great, I was going to need at least part of the money to stake it.

A Huge Chunk Of Money

"I started saving. At age 25 I only earned about $16,000 a year. But by the time I was 35 I had a huge chuck of money in the bank. I followed a simple savings plan that anyone can follow. I didn't wheel and deal. I disciplined myself. Every time I was tempted to spend money foolishly, I would picture my huge bulging bank account instead. This took away my desire to spend. Amassing that first chunk of money gave me tremendous confidence. It led to a big turning point.

In A Rocking Chair

"At 33 I was earning a good income and was considered successful by other people's standards. Yet I felt restless. I knew aviation wasn't the right work for me. I was hungry for something bigger that I could really get my teeth into. But I didn't know *what*. I used mental picturing to project myself into the future.

"I relaxed and imagined that I was 70 years old, sitting in a rocking chair and looking back over my life in the aviation industry. I did not like what I saw. Aviation did not have the heart and soul for what I wanted to do.

Anyone Can Succeed

"I wanted to help people break away from the limitations imposed on them by society. Like the teacher who said I would never set the world on fire. *Anyone can succeed.* The way you do this is to stop, relax and visualise your way forward. This will give you the courage and discipline to succeed. Then you can change. Most people push harder when they want to change their lives, but you need to 'chill out' and think if you want to create a turning point. I found mental picturing the consummate tool to do this.

A Billion Dollar Book

"While working for Aerotest Airways, I'd been working on the side to earn extra money. One of my projects was the book, **Billion Dollar Marketing** by Maxwell Sackheim I went from one book store to another to persuade them to stock my books. I discovered that the publishing industry was in *chaos*. This was my opportunity.

"Most books were being sold through book stores, but I did my homework and found out that only 18% of the American population ever enters a book store. That's 80% of the population that's not being served. That's a lot. It's a fortune. I knew I'd hit on my 'This is it!'—I decided to go into publishing and created my own company, Great Wisdom Publishing, Inc.

Knowledge Is Power

"Great Wisdom is dedicated to giving people the kind of information that *wakes them up* to their own power to change their lives. We'll do this by delivering top quality products to our customer's doorsteps.

"Every day I picture Great Wisdom as a blue chip company with a fine reputation. When we recommend a book, our customers will automatically buy it because they trust us. Fine companies exist like this and I want Great Wisdom to be one of them.

We Are All Self-Made

"People think that to be wealthy or influential, you have to be born into a wealthy, influential family. That's rubbish. We are all self-made. Most rich and influential people started from nothing. But they all had one thing in common—they all had rich dreams.

"The good forces would win..."

Chapter Three

Bob's Wolverines

In 1965 the American radiologist Dr. Carl Simonton pioneered the use of mental picturing as a powerful tool for curing cancer. One of his patients, Bob Gilley had a 30% chance of survival. As a last ditch attempt to recover, Gilley tried mental picturing.

"I'd begin to visualise my cancer" said Gilley, "as I saw it in my mind's eye. I'd make a game of it. The cancer would be a snake, a wolverine or some vicious animal. The cure? White husky dogs by the millions. It would be a confrontation of good and evil. I'd envision the dogs grab the cancer and shaking it, ripping it to shreds. The forces of good would win. The cancer would shrink from a big snake to a little snake and then disappear. Then the army of dogs would lick up the residue and clean my abdominal cavity until it was spotless."

Gilley pictured this scene three times a day for 10-15 minutes. After six weeks an examination revealed his tumour had shrunk by 75%. After two months Gilley had a cancer scan and there was no trace of the disease left in his body." (*New Age Journal, April 1974*). In the next chapter you'll see how Chris Banks used a similar technique.

13

Chris got rid of his death wish . . .

Chapter Four

Chris Conquered Cancer

"You're not going to make it. You'd better put your affairs in order and make a will. I'm sorry but your body is virtually riddled with cancer". Thirty-two year old junior accountant Chris Banks was diagnosed with terminal cancer and given three to five months to live.

"I felt trapped in a syndrome of 'just keeping up' " said Chris. "I was living this lunatic lifestyle of non-stop work, trying to act successful. But money was tight. And, here I was an accountant and supposed to know about money.

"I just could not keep up financially. I'd cut down on all my expenses and almost stopped eating in order to save. Meanwhile I was trying to put on a cheerful face and not let on that I was so hard up. It was murder.

"I fell into bed at night too exhausted to even change my cloths, I didn't shave. I was a mess. I felt like a total failure—a misfit. I became so depressed that I just could not see a future for myself. That's when they diagnosed cancer.

The Key

"Somewhere inside me though, I knew there was a happy, successful Chris trying to get out if only I could find the key. In a way cancer gave it to me.

"Even though the doctors gave me absolutely no hope I didn't 'cave in', I got angry instead. I got counselling and read everything I could about others who had recovered from terminal cancer. One thing they all shared in common was that they had practiced mental picturing.

"I read about mental picturing and started to practice it immediately. At first, I didn't really believe it would work, but the more I pictured, the more I realised I didn't *have* to die. I had a *choice*. The first thing I pictured was getting rid of my death-wish. And boy, did I enjoy it.

Chris Got Rid Of His Death Wish

"I didn't want to die," continued Chris, "it's just that I couldn't *see* living this way anymore. I was desperate for a way out. Through counselling I learned that I wouldn't be facing death unless somewhere along the line I'd consented to it. Not consciously of course, but a stranger can't walk through your front door unless you open it. I had unwittingly opened a door in my mind and accepted this as a way out. I immediately closed that door by destroying my so-called death wish and 'killed' two birds with one stone.

Shoot The Computer

"I hated my work and always had. I had always wanted to paint. But my parents and girl friend insisted that I couldn't make any money at it. I decided to show them.

"I relaxed and pictured my office, especially my computer. There were times when I felt so trapped sitting long hours at the computer screen, with piles of paper all over that I wanted to take the computer and throw it out the window. In my imagination, I did something better. I shot it. This may sound dramatic but it made me feel like a million.

"I took out an imaginary gun and shot my computer over and over. I shot it to smithereens. Then I shot all the stacks of papers, files, books, my desk and chair. As a last touch, I shot out all the windows of my office. No gangster movie could have done it better.

Insurance

"Then I collected. I imagined standing in the shambles that *was* my office, broken glass and papers everywhere. Then I pictured an insurance broker walk in and hand me a huge check for damages. I immediately spent part of it on art materials. Next I pictured taking a holiday, with no particular destination, except to go everywhere beautiful. I pictured myself sitting on the deck of a ship painting beautiful pictures.

"This mental picturing brought me surprising power and relief. It also inspired me to get more creative. I took up sketching and drawing and also started picturing for the future.

Picturing The Future

"I decided to picture being married and raising a family. So, in place of my old office I imagined a smiling wife in a garden where we were having a barbecue. We had two children, a boy and a girl romping on the grass. It was an idyllic scene.

"I always wanted children, but my girl friend was such a workaholic that she wouldn't consider starting a family. It really broke up our relationship. That and the

You can do it!

fact that she made so much more money than I did. The inadequacy I felt in our relationship was tangible. But the happiness I feel today is too."

Freedom From Cancer

Chris Banks has now been completely free from cancer for over five years. He lives in Kenya and pursues the painting career he always wanted and earns more money now than he ever did as an accountant. He's married and he and his wife are planning a family.

Says Chris, "Mental picturing gave me the confidence to heal myself. I decided against the radical surgery suggested by the doctors. I know they meant well but they didn't have to live with the consequences of radical surgery or treatments that would have left me semi-disabled." said Chris. "If a gentler, less intrusive solution was available I wanted to try it first. I learned everything possible about how to strengthen my immune system, followed a good diet and exercised.

"My diet consisted of simple, healthy foods and *plenty of them*. It was clear I had been virtually starving myself for years. I drank copious quantities of fresh vegetable and fruit juices which gave me high energy, took vitamin supplements and ate plenty of protein. I opted for imuno-therapy instead of surgery. And of course, I followed a *full* diet of positive mental picturing daily." said a broadly smiling and obviously healthy Chris.

Nip It In The Bud

When Chris learned mental picturing was crucial to his success. Illness and 'the threat of death' go through three stages: denial, anger and resignation. Catching an illness (or poverty, loneliness etc.) in its early stages of denial and anger helps mental picturing work faster, because you've got plenty of fight in you.

It's simple. If you spilled a cup of black coffee all over your pale carpet, would you wait until the stain had sunk in and completely dried before cleaning it up? Of course not, you would jump and clean it up right away.

The same goes for any illness. Catch it early and get rid of it fast. When illness (or any problem) reaches the resignation stage, you need dynamite to dislodge it. But it isn't hopeless. Winston Churchill said, "Never give up! Never, *never* give up." When a dire situation threatens you or those you love — *fight. Don't give up.* We fight for such silly things, then something 'big' like cancer or bankruptcy comes along and we give in.

Fight With Your Mind, Not With Your Fists

Chris fought and won. He learned how to *heal himself.*
There is a big difference between healing yourself and
turning your body over to someone else to do it. Why?
No one feels comfort or discomfort in your body more
than you do. Therefore, no one is a better judge of
'what feels right' than you are. Each person has a
different body chemistry, likes, dislikes and energy
level. What heals one will not heal another.

This doesn't mean to say that you should flaunt
medical advice. But don't swallow it whole either.
Chris' doctors lost patience with him when he didn't
jump at their suggested treatments. But gradually as
they saw him learn, inform himself and participate in
his own healing they came to respect him.

Mobilize A Mental Army

It helped that Chris had a sense of humour. How
many could shoot a computer and enjoy it so? Chris
grinned, "I gave all my friends a book on mental
picturing and asked them to visualise for me instead of
worrying. I virtually mobilized a mental army. And we
won."

The Egyptians left nothing to chance. They planned...

Chapter Five

Chart Your Future

Egyptian kings and queens in 3,000 B.C. planned glorious futures for their children by painting all the dreams they had for them on the walls their palaces and tombs. Wall paintings charted futures full of wealth, rich harvests, wise teachers, beautiful palaces, protective gods, music, noble partners, healthy bodies and thriving kingdoms.

When that child became an adult, married and eventually died, mental picturing was again used. The tomb was furnished with gold, grain, honey, linens, scented oils, and even servants. In fact everything *imaginable* the deceased would need for a blissful afterlife.

The Egyptians left nothing to chance. They planned...

You can plan too through mental picturing. In the next chapter you will see how Susie Harris like the Egyptians, combined her designing skills with mental picturing to land herself a dream job.

*Every day Susie walked through the fabric department
and pictured how it would look when she ran it...*

Chapter Six

Susie Harris' Golden Road

"I was determined." said Susie Harris, 40, textile controller at the famous Liberty department store in London. "After my divorce I wanted a complete break from my old lifestyle and tried many different careers. I learned reflexology, led self-confidence workshops and even tried photography but nothing seemed to work. Money was tight and I was getting deeply worried. I decided to work out my future through mental picturing.

"I didn't go out and look for a job. I first pictured what I wanted my job to be. I wanted to improve peoples lives by giving them beautiful things they would adore. I also wanted to travel. I sat down with a big sheet of paper and my daughter Laura's coloured pens and drew my dream job. The first thing I drew was a beautiful golden road which I surrounded with beautiful objects, people, aeroplanes, plenty of money and a loving, relationship.

What I Do Best

"As a result of vividly picturing my future I realised

clearly why things had not been working for me. I had been resisting my own true talents. Before my husband and I divorced, we ran a textile company; after my divorce I wanted a completely new lifestyle and career. But I realised, *I was denying what I do best.*

"I'm a creative, tactile person and working with textiles gave me that fulfilment. I made a decision—I was going back into textiles. All the rest fell into place. I made a few phone calls to people in the industry then I went out and bought a trade journal. I opened to the classified ads and '*saw*' my dream job. Liberty was looking for a textile controller. I knew the job was mine.

Picturing Plus Practice

"That didn't mean getting it was easy though. There were a hundred applicants. I really had to put my mental picturing to the acid test. Every day I spent a couple of hours walking through the fabric department of Liberty picturing how it would look when I ran it. I mentally pictured myself at each successive interview making a good impression. Through that mental picturing, I became so determined that nothing could stop me.

"I got the job which brought me more fulfilment than I ever imagined. I always use mental picturing at work. If we're working on a new collection, I first mentally picture how everything will look completed, then I go out and select the fabrics. I have many of the fabrics designed exactly as I've pictured them.

My Next Step

"As a result the fabric department has grown, I have been promoted and my relationship with Liberty has flourished. I am now setting up my own textile consultancy, **McLaren And Associates** to produce textiles and other beautiful coordinating products. I will continue working with Liberty and with other new clients who are already approaching me.

"Why did I choose the name McLaren? That's the name of my new husband. Robert and I married on the 14th of February of this year. Remember, a loving relationship was an *important* part of my 'Golden Road'.

Nothing Is Beyond Reach

"Since learning mental picturing I have never looked back; it has become second nature. Sometimes I have to pinch myself because I know I've created all these successes and can create more."

This Goes For You

You too can use mental picturing to land yourself a dream job the way Susie Harris did; or to achieve anything else you want. You and I never fail because we lack opportunity or ability. We fail because we're not certain about what we want. Or, we know what we want, but feel it is beyond our reach.

Nothing is beyond your reach when you use mental picturing. The very act of picturing your desires *wakes up* your *subconscious mind*. Your subconscious holds all the solutions about how to get what you want. You contact it every time your picture a positive future goal. The way your subconscious communicates with you is by triggering ideas within your *conscious* mind to show you how to achieve it.

You'll Get Ideas

When Susie Harris drew her 'Golden Road' and pictured her dream job, she got an idea to go out and buy a trade journal and bingo, there was her job—

advertised in the classified's. Then she pictured herself landing the job and got the idea to walk the fabric department every day in order to see how to improve it. As a result, when she went into an interview she was fully prepared. She had researched the fabric department, could speak intelligently about it and make positive suggestions. *She had done her homework.*

Don't Throw It All Away

The reason Susie had been in a career standstill before she designed her 'Golden Road' was a due to common mistake we all make. Because we fail in one area, we feel that everything else we've done is wrong.

Susie's marriage failed and it made her feel that her career had been a mistake too. So, she determined to start fresh by doing something completely new.

Haven't we all done this? We think that because one part of our life has failed, that it's all wrong. But if the clutch on your car wears out, you don't throw out the whole motor and brakes and other parts. You just fix the clutch. The same applies to your life. When a career, relationship or your health fails, just fix the part that's failed. Don't throw everything out!

*Eye-witnesses have seen Buddhists melt snow they
are sitting in through mental picturing...*

Chapter Seven

Mind Bending

Susie Harris used mental picturing to achieve something glamourous, but young Buddhist monks use it to escape dire straits. In the dead of winter they are locked out of their temples overnight and made to sit naked in the snow in order to pass their initiation ceremonies. They have one thing to keep them warm: their mind. They picture a hot burning sun inside their body to stay warm. If they fail they freeze. If they succeed, they become monks. The initiates not only stay warm, but eye-witnesses report they melt all the snow around them.

The actress, Shirley MacLaine used a similar technique when travelling high in the Andes mountains of Peru. She had to sleep through the freezing night with only a native Peruvian poncho to keep her warm. She stayed warm by mentally picturing a hot tropical sun beating down on her. To her amazement she stared sweating so profusely she had to throw her poncho off.

These are mind-bending accounts. But what if you and I want something more comforting like a loving relationship? Can mental picturing work for this?

*Christina had succeeded as a businesswoman
and mother; now it was time for her...*

Chapter Eight

Christina Found Her Man

"Something was missing from my life." said Christina Bachini 49, mother of two who divorced in 1970 and had not had a steady relationship for years. After achieving a diploma in humanistic psychology at Surrey University in England in l989, Christina began coaching stress management, communication skills, and assertiveness to people from all walks of life.

"I became fascinated by what it is that enables some people to achieve what they want while others fail. Many people feel "I'm the way I am and I can't change." But that's not true. I found mental picturing a fine tool for creating positive change. I formed my own company called Chrysalis to enable people to make a complete change in their lives when they come to a crossroads and don't know which way to turn.

My Next Success-Step

"Despite my success, something was missing. In 1994 I went to a seminar and realised that what I really wanted was a relationship. I had really succeed as a mother and in my career. Now I realised the next step was to succeed in a relationship. I'd grown as much as I could without one.

"I read a story in the book **Chicken Soup For The Soul** about a woman who had made a scrapbook of all the qualities she wanted in a man and mentally pictured them every day by leafing through the book. I didn't make a scrap book, instead I wrote a detailed list. I was more interested in my new man's internal qualities than I was in his external ones. This was my list:

Christina's List

1. His height — I wanted a man who was tall.

2. Well built — body structure is very important to me so he had to be in good shape physically.

3. No particular eye colour as long as his eyes were kind and intelligent.

4. He had to have good teeth.

5. He had to be interested in my work, or be involved in human development so we could

communicate on the same wave length.

6. He had to have a generous spirit, willingness to share and sense of fun.

7. He had to *really* love me. That means for who I am with all my good points as well as my 'warts'.

8. Lastly, he had to be honest and absolutely monogamous so I would feel safe in the relationship and continue to grow and develop personally.

Pictured Every Day

"Every day I pictured each item on my list. Nothing much happened except that I began to feel relaxed, confident and certain that the relationship would soon materialise. I had no desire to go out look and 'look for a man', I had found him in my heart.

"One day I received a brochure in the mail advertising a training course in Canada. I drove to work and thought, 'I'm going on that seminar, it can teach me something'. I went to the seminar and feel deeply in love with Hugh Smith.

"When I first saw Hugh in the seminar I said, "You're looking very grumpy." Hugh said, "That's because I'm looking for someone to play with. I said, 'You can play with me.' It just popped out, I *never* say things like that. Hugh invited me to go cycling the next morning at 7:30. We stopped to have coffee I started to talk and told him some personal things. He was completely supportive and I realised I could completely open up to him. In that moment I believe I fell in love.

A Perfect Partner

Hugh Smith, 43, is a perfect partner for Christina emotionally and for work as well. A retired vice president of Cor States Bank in Philadelphia, Hugh specialised in Total Quality Engineering to motivate employees to offer the highest quality product to the customer. Hugh and Christina now run workshops together on performance, relationships and stress which feature mental picturing.

"We are in a totally committed partnership. The more we're together, the more difficult it is to be apart. The thing we miss is being on the same side of the Atlantic Ocean, but we're mentally picturing to solve that problem now. We both know we will get what we want we're just not sure when", says Christina smiling.

What Makes You Tick?

"Where can I find a man. Where can I find a man?"
How often have you heard women say this? Or,
perhaps you have said it yourself. Men say the same
about women.

The place you find your ideal partner is in your heart.
You find him (or her) in your heart by analysing what
makes you tick and what you need in a relationship to
become more of who you really are. Then your partner
will materialise in your life.

Rich?

Very often women want a 'rich husband'. But rich in
what? Money? A man who is only rich in money isn't
going to be much of a soul-mate. How about finding a
man who is rich in every way? Sit down and write your
list the way Christina did. This goes for men too.
Fellows have just as much trouble finding partners as
women.

Remember what you liked most about your other
relationships. Every relationship had its strong, positive
points. What were they? When you analyse what you
loved about someone, you'll see how they helped you

and taught you great lessons. If you'll value the lessons they taught you, you won't feel jilted or as if you failed. Then you can use mental picturing to find your next mate.

Act

Christina didn't go out and 'look' for a man. She didn't have to because mental picturing made her feel confident and secure her man was on the way. Sure enough, she received the brochure, she felt right about it and she *acted* on her positive feeling.

She went to the seminar never guessing that she'd meet Hugh. Mental picturing works only when you *act* on your ideas. Then, when you least expect it, your dream will come true.

Anthropoligist's Note

Anthropoligists have studied in detail what it is that attracts people to each other. Men are usually drawn to women with curvaceous bodies, good confidence and and good health. This is because men traditionally (even though this is changing) act as providers and look for women who can manage a home, produce offspring and care for the family (including the man!).

Women on the other hand, even when they have a good income of their own, look for a man who is a good provider. This is one of their *'big ones'*. Studies reveal that a woman's natural instinct is to nurture. One can't easily nurture a family and provide for them at the same time. A friend aptly put it this way: "I want a man who is a little older, a little wiser and a little richer than me." She found him.

The Clinchers

In the final analysis, anthropologists report that the two qualities that *clinch* long term relationships between men and women are not money, good looks, sex or fame. The qualities couples 'fall for' in each other are *kindness and intelligence.*

Run your fingers through the gold...

Chapter Nine

Mental Movies

Mental picturing is the art of creating 'mental movies' for yourself and then *acting them out* as if they were *real*. That's what the Ice Age cave dwellers did when they stared at pictures of animals they wanted to hunt and then speared them. It's what Susie Harris did when she walked through the fabric department of Liberty and pictured how it would look when she ran it. It's what other people in this book did. It's what you will do when you set your mind to succeed. You'll create, rehearse, act-out and produce a whole new future for yourself. And, your life will change.

Happy Endings, Not Nightmares

Everything you've pictured up until now has made up your life as you know it today. By the same token, everything you picture from now on will create your future. Decide right now that your future is going to be a good luck story not a horror film. However, in case you find yourself trapped in a nightmare situation, mental picturing offers a quick escape.

Mike blew the troublemaker out of the boat...

Chapter Ten

Mike Saved The Show

"It was really painful. At a thousand dollars a minute when you get a control-freak messing up a film shoot, it just destroys everyone."

California television producer Mike Lestico, 49 was at the end of his tether when an executive for an ad agency representing his client turned out to be a control-freak who ordered everyone around. "The sense of fun and adventure that permeates our location shoots had disintegrated." said Mike.

"This fellow didn't have the technical knowledge or the hands-on skill to deal with people and he knew it. To compensate he started telling everyone how to do their job and the result was chaos, disruptions and hard feelings. He was upsetting the talent, telling the camera people what to do. He didn't know enough to let us do our job."

The budget for the popular adventure-travel t.v. series 'Great Sports Vacations' was going out of control and crew morale was low. Mike had to act quickly.

Blow It Up

In one of my books Mike had read about how you can use mental picturing to destroy a difficult situation. This is a technique where you relax, close your eyes and picture a difficult problem or a 'troublemaker' and blow them up. Techniques that destroy never cause harm they just clear the air and get rid of problems.

"It was either blow this guy up in my imagination, or blow up *myself* in *reality*. I was furious. Here we were, on location in a foreign country, cast and crew confined on a boat in the open water in the sea of Cortez. I felt trapped like a rat in a can. My back was against the wall. I had to turn the situation around and decided to give mental picturing a try.

Mike Relaxed

"I walked to the back of the boat, sat down, got comfortable and put my feet up. I closed my eyes, took a deep breath and tried to enjoy the cool breeze and warm sun. Then I started picturing. I repeatedly blew this guy up in my imagination. Soon I started to chuckle. Then I began to laugh. Eventually I was laughing so hard I had to stop picturing.

"I got up and walked to the front of the boat feeling incredibly relaxed and, trying to keep a straight face, I gave this guy two jobs. *I just knew what to do.* The jobs made him feel important and also helped me.

Sort Out The Cops

"First, we had a problem with the local police who were giving us a hard time about our filming permits, so I let him sort that problem out. I also told him that I really needed someone to rehearse the actors. He did both jobs well, it kept him out of the way and the rest of the film-shoot went off without a hitch." Mike's programme turned out to be a great success and to his delight even ran under budget.

"Getting along with the cast and clients on location is crucial to the quality of the end product not just the budget." says Mike. We make it a practice to always enjoy going out on location to shoot a new episode. But this time it was murder. Mental picturing broke the grip of my fury. I honestly think techniques that destroy are some of the most valuable you can use. Blowing up that guy really cleared the air."

Office Politics

Enjoyment and professionalism work hand in hand in any successful project. Office politics can be stressful when you are trying to do a job well. Whether you work for a large company or are an independent like Mike, amateurish, petty people can get foisted on you with whom you have to work and get along. If you have high standards it can make work a nightmare. If someone or something is obstructing the congenial flow, techniques that destroy are invaluable.

Get Even Safely

Mike was so furious he was ready to 'blow up'. By blowing up the troublemaker in his imagination he accomplished three empowering things. First, he vented his fury and 'got even' safely instead of having an all-out battle with the ad agency executive. Second, he controlled the situation and gave his subconscious mind an opportunity to communicate constructive solutions to him. As Mike said, "After picturing I just *knew* what to do. I gave the guy two jobs." Third, he gave this difficult person an opportunity to contribute constructively to the project, which made him feel valuable and as if he fit in.

"I turned a potential disaster into success through about 10 minutes of mental picturing. As painful as it was this was a valuable experience because it taught me how mental picturing can control a difficult situation without an ugly confrontation. It's absolutely empowering." said Mike.

Keep The Cash Flowing

"Next, I solved our cash flow problems. The nature of our business is that we work on large projects and can go months without a deal. There are times when the cash flow gets very tight and and it puts everyone under a strain. I decided to try mental picturing.

"I'd read how picturing yourself walking on money or wearing gold shoes will bring in extra cash. I decided to give it a try. Every time I walked my dog I would picture walking on piles of money and wearing gold shoes. I imagined a bulging bank account.

"What happened next was incredible. A week later money started flying in from everywhere, even unexpected places. It wasn't that I was working harder either. If anything, I was working less. Now I always picture for cash flow. It sure relieves the pressure."

"I saw the branch as <u>not</u> breaking..."

Chapter Eleven

Reverse Disaster

You are always picturing. If I describe the beautiful sunset I saw on my holiday, even though you weren't with me you automatically picture a sunset in your mind. You mentally drift off and picture a vast, radiant sky and imagine you're there. You may murmur 'Uhm..' and take a sigh of pleasure. Just for a moment, you took my holiday.

The same holds true if I describe to you a dreadful scene, for instance an automobile accident with police cars, ambulances and flashing lights. You tense up, get butterflies in your stomach and feel "Oh, what if that happened to *me*." Your heart may even start pounding as you imagine the accident. Mine is, as I write this. You take another sigh of relief thinking "Thank heavens, the accident didn't happen to me."

But it did. Maybe you didn't get a broken leg or arm but briefly you lived that accident *with deep involvement.* Can you walk away from an accident a winner? Rarely. But you can escape the worst if you'll live your escape with deep involvement.

49

Greg fell asleep picturing himself backpacking...

Chapter Twelve

Greg Healed His Broken Arms

The following story is personal, but I would like to include it because the 'close call' and quick escape still boggle my imagination. I also learned how important 'talking it out' is to recover from a physical trauma.

When my son Greg was twenty he decided to travel through Africa for a year of back-packing. Three weeks before he was to depart he took our two dogs for a run in the woods of Hampton Court in England, nearby where we lived.

To test out some of his camping gear he decided to climb a tree. His boots gripped the tall, ancient oak tree fine, but what he didn't know until it was too late, was that the next branch he stepped on was completely rotten. His foot shot through the branch, he completely lost his balance and hurtled to the ground 30 feet below.

"When I opened my eyes and saw the sky I thought, 'Boy, am I glad this didn't happen in Africa where rescue services are nil'." said Greg.

"The dogs jumped and barked around me but I could barely move. Somehow I managed to get up, but I couldn't use my arms or hands and walking was difficult. I called to someone walking in the woods and asked them to help me. They picked up my gear and took me and our dogs to the game-keepers cottage to get help. First the police came, then an ambulance took me to Kingston hospital. The police took the dogs home where my mother was working." said Greg.

I Went Cold

When the police arrived I, Julia went cold. I was in the middle of coaching a client when there was a knock at the door. The police said "There's been a little accident, your son is in emergency. We have your two dogs in our car." The word *little* made my stomach turn over.

The police were non-committal about Greg's injuries. Deep down, I knew he was o.k. because I always pictured him happy and healthy. But at the same time, I was panicked. My client left, I fed the dogs and left immediately for the hospital. For what seemed like hours I waited to see Greg. It took effort, but I visualised the whole time, picturing Greg smiling and hearing him say, "Mom, don't worry. I'm fine!"

Two Broken Arms

Finally the nurses let me see Greg. The minute I saw his smile I knew he was o.k., but I also knew from the way he was sitting that he was injured. We sat and talked and he told me what happened. We met with the doctor who diagnosed a fractured wrist on the right hand and a fractured elbow on the left. The nurses dressed both Greg's arms in plaster casts, gave him pain pills and assured us that Greg needed at *least* 6-8 weeks in plaster casts. Nothing less.

Greg Talked Into The Night

Not having eaten since breakfast Greg was ravenous for cheeseburgers, french fries and a chocolate shake. It sounds like a whim, but after a physical trauma the body craves sugar, salt and fat to perk it up.

We bought the food, went home and eased Greg into a chair. Stunned, I fed him bite by bite and listened while he talked late into the night. Greg described over and over what had happened. He talked until he had talked himself out.

As he talked, something we had both noticed in the hospital happened again: the swelling in his hands and arms reduced before our eyes. There was something about talking that alleviated the swelling. I later learned the body holds water under stress in order to keep the blood pressure and heartbeat steady. But as the body relaxes (which Greg's did as he talked) water retention (in this case the swelling) disperses.

I said, "Greg, you're leaving for Africa in three weeks for a year of backpacking. You can't go in plaster casts. What can you do?" We decided to visualise. Greg went to sleep and we propped his arms on pillows. As he drifted off he pictured all the cells in his arms knitting together and becoming stronger. He imagined *being in Africa* and hoisting up his backpack with strong arms.

It Didn't Happen

I tried a different tactic and visualised the whole scene just as he had described it but as *not* happening. I sat on the living room sofa and over and over, pictured Greg climb up the tree and climb down again. I *saw* him step on the rotten branch, but instead, I pictured the branch strong and able to support him. Then I pictured him walking in the front door smiling broadly at the end of a great day.

An Ace Up Our Sleeve

We visualised daily, morning and night. About ten days later Greg said, "O.K., you can cut these casts off." I gulped, but cut them off because I knew we had an ace up our sleeves. It was a float tank. This is a large enclosed bathtub filled with warm water saturated with epson salts. You float effortlessly, like a cork on the sea and *nothing* accelerates healing quite so fast when you combine it with mental picturing. Greg floated every day and pictured his arms getting stronger and stronger.

The story has a completely happy end. Greg departed for Africa, his backpack on his back, jammed with a year's supply of equipment. The weight of thing was phenomenal. One push and he would have toppled over. He travelled through Africa for a year, once got malaria, dysentery, mugged, robbed and even shot at in a revolution, but his arms never bothered him.

Even to me as I write it now, Greg's story seems impossible. But it happened exactly as I have recounted. The only thing Greg and I are sorry about is that we never went back to the Kingston hospital to get final X-rays.

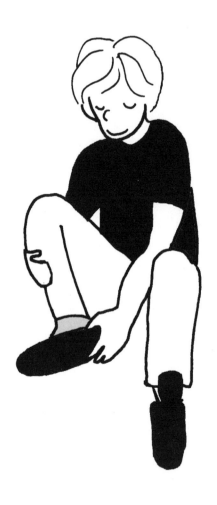

I don't want to be lonely...

Chapter Thirteen

Kids Today Are Scared

"Young people growing up today have fear-based goals whereas *before* they had *aspirations*." says Rory Jeffes, Chief Executive of 'The Site', an award-winning internet site set up by BBC newscaster Martyn Lewis to help young people learn about the enormous opportunities available to them when they leave school.

"Fifteen years ago, kids had lofty aims" says Rory. "They took it for granted they would live in a nice home, have a partner and family they could be proud of, a good job and smart car. Now the climate has changed. They're scared. Young people today have three fear-based goals: they don't want to be unemployed, they don't want to be homeless and they don't want to be lonely."

Goals And Aspirations

Goals are different from aspirations. Aspirations are lofty hopes and dreams. While goals always *start* with a dream, they become a one-step-at-a-time process that gets you ahead. If you want to get ahead in today's world when companies no longer offer 'jobs for life', you need the courage to stick to your goals and believe in your dreams. Rick Ospina found both in mental picturing.

They said Rick would never make anything of his life. He proved them all wrong...

Chapter Fourteen

Rick Got It Together

At age 14, Colombian born Rick Ospina was homeless, unemployed and so lonely he was suicidal. What's more, no one gave him a chance at happiness. "He's rebellious and impossible." said his social worker. "If he ever makes anything out of his life it will be a miracle." Yet Rick did make something of his life.

Today at 30, Rick can't lose for winning. He's married and owns his own home in a smart Minneapolis suburb. He and his wife Tiffany love each other deeply and spend every possible moment together. Rick is a successful real estate agent and property developer. His happiness is so contagious it's just good to be around him. It's difficult to believe he ever had a problem.

Foster Homes

Starting from age 13, Rick was placed in one foster home after another because he was so rebellious. "I wasn't rebellious, it's just that I was a dreamer and wanted to make my own decisions. Kids are very sensitive to being dismissed. But when you're small, you just don't realise how hard your parents are trying.

"I ran away from my third foster home at age 15 and hitchhiked to Georgia. I had $5 in my pocket and lived off that and telling my stories. People were incredibly kind when they heard what I'd been through. They fed me and gave me clothing and shelter.

"The authorities finally caught up with me, brought me back to the Twin Cities and placed me in another foster home. It didn't last long, after a couple of weeks I got kicked out. By the time I was 16, I was formally placed in foster care and sent to an outward bound, 'Boys Town' kind of camp. We had to work hard. We were on an honour system and got points for doing our tasks well. One time we had to walk 80 miles in 8 days on snow shoes. Actually, it was a great experience. After that, I tried college, hoping it could put me on the right track, but I soon got kicked out of there too.

Suicidal

"That's when I became suicidal again. At my absolute lowest ebb I took an overdose. When I recovered from the coma, I tried going home to live with my parents, but we always ended up arguing. I was a *very* mixed up kid. I left home to share an apartment with some heavy-drinking drifters. The whole scene was so degrading and depressing that, again I became suicidal.

I Let Go Of Self-Pity

"I was sitting on the sofa figuring out *how* I would kill myself when something happened. It was like a bubble burst. I 'saw' myself getting up off the sofa, getting a job and making a career on my own. It was an incredibly vivid experience that completely changed my life. I realised I *had* to stop feeling sorry for myself. *It is the greatest lesson anyone can learn.*

"Every day I visualised the same scene: getting up off the sofa and going out and getting a job. Then I pounded the pavements. As I was walked, I pictured myself driving a new car instead. I pictured owning a nice, clean home and having a wonderful partner. One night on a double date I met Tiffany. It was instant recognition for both of us and we married soon after. Tiffany made me look deeply at myself. The deeper I looked the more ambitions I became.

"I finally landed a job collecting student loans and was very good at it. I was offered a promotion but decided to go into real estate. Helping people find homes is incredibly satisfying. My clients often come back and ask me to negotiate other deals for them: land in other countries, boats, jewellry, in fact anything they want to buy. I have a solid reputation which I owe to three things: letting go of self-pity, always keeping my word, and *continuous mental picturing.*"

In 6,000 B.C. the Greeks were using mental picturing...

Chapter Fifteen

Famous Greeks

The Greek philosopher Aristotle said, "The mind cannot think without pictures." Indeed, it can't. The Greeks were were famous for their healing temples where mental picturing played an important part in the cure, whether the problem was hard luck, jealously, poverty, illness or a broken bone. Patients often travelled from great distances to be healed.

Temples were beautiful. They had dormitories, gyms, libraries, immaculate gardens, baths, theatres, stadiums and of course, shrines for the healing God Asklepious.

The patient's first step was to take a bath, then go on a special diet and next to visit the shrine of Asklepious to ask the god for favour. In the evening the patient was dressed in white and sent to a special room to sleep. Once the patient was asleep, priests dressed in costumes went into the room and described healing pictures to the patient while he slept. As a result, the patient had vivid dreams and often experienced complete healings. This technique is almost identical to that used by most hypnotherapists today.

"I 'saw' a series of books in my mind...."

Chapter Sixteen

Lynn's Career Breakthrough

Lynn Palmer bubbles with enthusiasm. But not long ago her career was at a standstill. "It was as if I was always in pain, either emotionally or physically. My neck and back ached. So did my head. I don't know if my aches and pains made me depressed, or the other way around, but I felt stuck.

"I attended a seminar in mental picturing in April '96. The workshop sounded too good to be true but I thought, 'What have I got to loose?' I had heard others were changing their lives through mental picturing and decided to give it a try.

Amazed

"I was *amazed*. Very quickly many good things happened that I never expected to happen. First I pictured being in great health and feeling really happy. Almost immediately I felt a lift in my mood. The pain in my neck and back improved so much I was able to stop taking pain killers. That gave me enormous confidence.

"By a lucky chance I found a hypnotherapist who specialised in mental picturing and started working with her. She projected me into my ideal future and showed me how to apply mental picturing to speed things up. The feeling of optimism I experienced as a result was a turning point. Life really opened up for me. What's more, I *knew* I was opening those doors."

A New Car

Lynn continued enthusiastically, "I decided to try mental picturing on more things, the next being a new car. We owned a Volvo wagon which was too difficult for me to drive. I wanted a car with power steering. One day I saw a Volvo sports car and thought, "That's nice. I'll mentally picture diving one of those.

"One month later, my husband brought home that exact same car as a surprise for me. He didn't even know I had been picturing it. It's the *perfect car,* easy to drive, light, and most importantly exactly what I wanted. And, all I had to do was picture it. I didn't even have to buy it, my husband did.

A Holiday

"My next picturing success was a wonderful holiday in

Spain. My husband and I longed to stay at a hotel we had stayed at before, but because I was out of work, couldn't afford. I decided to picture us taking the holiday anyway and staying at exactly that hotel.

"Each day I mentally pictured walking on the beach in front of the hotel and paddling in the warm water. Out of the blue, good friends telephoned to say they'd located an apartment right next door to this hotel at half the price. By splitting the rent with our friends, it cost us next to nothing and we had a wonderful time. As I walked by the sea in front of 'the hotel' and paddled in the warm water, I inwardly smiled at how magically my luck had turned.

The Breakthrough

"Then my big mental picturing breakthrough came. My career may have been at a standstill but every day I felt more like a winner. All my successes had brought back my confidence, and with it my creativity.

"I knew I wanted to write. My husband and I had written travel articles before, but I wanted to write imaginative stories for children. My grandson gave me the idea. One day I was teasing him and said "You're a little monkey." He said, "No, I'm not. I'm a Little Red

Tiger." A bell rang. That was the title for a series. I just
'saw' a whole series of children's books in my mind. My
husband and I have already written our first Little Red
Tiger book which goes on sale next year.

Money No Longer A Worry

"My list is endless about how mental picturing has
changed my life. No, that's not quite true. Mental
picturing has shown *me* how *I* can change my life. I
will never give it up.

"Money had been such a *draining* worry for so long,
but it's now flowing in again. I am getting more work,
so is my husband and we are both working at 'The
Tiger' books in our spare time. My relationships have
all improved... What more can I say? I used to wake up
every morning thinking, "Oh no, it's another day. Now
I wake up wondering what day will bring. It's a new
world for me."

A String Of Successes

Lynn's story of colourful successes shows how, just like
dominos you line up and push over, a stream of 'lucky
breaks' came her way. And she *knew* it was due to her
mental picturing.

The reason people feel such confidence as a result of their mental picturing is because, simply, the things they picture *happen*. They succeed.

Lynn had lost her confidence and needed this string of successes to restore it. She woke up to her own ability to make things happen. Once she had tasted success over and over, she got her big creative breakthrough, the Little Red Tiger Books. Using her imagination to inspire children through her writing has brought Lynn deep joy. The writing is her long-term career.

Lynn's confidence today is as high as it once was low. She says "I finally feel there's a wonderful future ahead. What a difference from before. I feel real self-esteem."

Your 'Golden Road' may be simple or
jam-packed with goodies...

Chapter Seventeen

Your Golden Road

Chart your 'Golden Road'. You can do this various ways: you can get a big piece of paper and draw your road the way Susie Harris did. Or, like David Reecher, you may enjoy sitting in a rocking chair looking back over your road now that you've 'made it'. You can write a detailed list of everything that's on your road the way Christina did to find her man.

No-Doubt-About-It

The road is your future. It belongs to you. Your road may be huge and sweeping, or it could be straight like a super highway. Design it any way you wish. Be sure to put *only* things you want on your road—the 'no-doubt-about-it' things you're sure about. You may put only a car, a palm tree or your cat. You may be surprised at how simple your road is. Or, you may be stunned that it's jam-packed with goodies.

Once you've drawn your road, either on paper or in your imagination, start picturing it.

It's easy...

Chapter Eighteen

Making It Happen

In the preceding chapters you've seen how from the Ice Age cave dwellers up until now, people have successfully used mental picturing to achieve their goals. Their goals were all different. But they all had one thing in common: their goals were crucial to their happiness and success.

Those who shared their stories for this book had their own 'nuts to crack'. Some were stuck in a standstill, others had their backs against the wall. They all succeeded. It was mental picturing that pulled them through.

- ❖ David made a million
- ❖ Christina got her man
- ❖ Susie and Lynn landed dream jobs
- ❖ Chris and Greg got well
- ❖ Mike and Rick got even

They all made money more easily. So can you. My other books go into the 'how to's' of mental picturing which can be elaborate or simple. For now, let's keep it simple.

Mental picturing is the art of training your mind to see the best. It will turn you into a natural positive thinker. Take these 3 steps and you will achieve your goals.

Decide on what you want
Picture what you want
Act on your ideas about how to make it happen

✤ Decide

Set aside 10-15 minutes each day, preferably in the morning. Sit down, relax and decide what you want. Don't think dedicating relax-time to yourself is being self-indulgent. It's an investment in your future.

To decide, make a list of everything you think you want whether it's a new house, a wonderful partner, a healthy body or a huge bank balance.

What You Don't Want

If you're not sure of what you want, list everything you don't want. This may seem negative, but it will help you make choices. For instance, you could list:

I don't want struggle. I want _____instead.

I don't want poverty. I want _____ instead.

I don't want loneliness. I want _____ instead.

The more complete you make your list, the more you'll learn about yourself. Leafing through magazines can give you ideas. Cut out pictures and make a scrap book of your no-doubt-about-it goals. Then picture them.

For instance, one could be of a great looking office and a shiny new car. These represent success and respect. Another could be a couple taking a first class cruise, or a lovely house in the country. It's fine to have a list of ten or more items.

♣ Picture

Picture each item on your list each day. If you want a smart office, imagine you're working in one. If it's a certain make of car, picture yourself driving one. If you want that cruise, smell the salt air... If you want a prestigious job, picture yourself in plush offices.

Picture each item on your list every day as if it were real right now. Taste, touch, smell, hear and feel each scene. Don't worry if you can't see like a photograph in your mind (I can't), just imagine as powerfully as you can.

Reinforce your mental pictures by affirming "I can have that." Put cards with positive statements written on them in places where you will see them often. For instance "I now have a great new job at great pay" on the dashboard of your car. Or, "I now have a loving relationship."

♣ Act

Once you've decided and pictured, then completely drop your mental picturing and go about your everyday activities. You'll start to trigger ideas within your own mind about how to achieve what you want.

Mental picturing is like having a conversation with your best friend, in this case the friend is your subconscious mind. Your subconscious knows your circumstances intimately and will communicate the best solutions suited to your present circumstances.

If you want to lose weight but you don't have two pennies to rub together, your subconscious won't give you an idea to go on a diet of grilled lamb chops, fresh asparagus and strawberries. It will give you an idea that won't blow your budget, like walking or bicycling to work instead of taking the bus, train or driving.

You may 'dream' how to achieve your goals like the ancient Greeks did. Or, you may get an idea to read the classified ads to find a new job like Susie Harris did.

Your subconscious will also communicate with you through other people. For instance, a friend may invite you to join them at an assertiveness workshop after you've been picturing to feel more self-confident.

Mental picturing works hand-in-hand with action. It takes very little discipline to develop this new success skill. And when you see how quickly the positive results start rolling in, like the people mentioned in this book, you'll never give it up. *You will have discovered within your own mind the master key to creating the future you want.*

If you would like more detailed information about how to practice mental picturing, my books, You're Great!, 3 Steps To Self-Confidence and The Day Dream Diet go into the fine points of this technique. For information on books see page 80.

Contacting Julia Hastings

Julia is always happy to hear from you. If you would like
to contact any of the people mentioned in this book you
can do this through Touchstone Publications. If you
would like to share your success story, your thoughts
about mental picturing or wish prompt mail order of
books or information about one-to-one coaching or
seminars; write to Julia at:

Touchstone Publications
518 19th Ave., N. E., Mlps., Mn., 55418, USA
WWW.You-Have-What-It-Takes.com
E-Mail:
Julia@ You-Have-What-It-Takes.com.

Coaching In Mental Picturing

One-to-one coaching in mental picturing is geared at
high-achievers. It's also useful for those who are ready
to make the leap into a fuller career or more
committed personal lifestyle.

Mental picturing first became known in sports when
the East German and Russian athletes used it to excel
in the Olympics. Golfers and skiers are known mental
picturers. This technique is now being used in
business, health care and education. The use of mental
picturing to accelerate the attainment of goals is
unparalleled.

You Are Always Picturing

"How often do you say "I knew it!" when something turns out the way you thought it would? Without realising it you are rehearsing an event *before* it happens. This is mental picturing."
You Can Have What You Want © Julia Hastings

The problem is that we often picture events we worry might happen instead of using our imagination to shape the events we want to have happen. Mental picturing will teach you how to do this. It will give you the tools to achieve a seamless transition to peak performance. You can contact Julia about one-to-one coaching visit our Web Site **WWW.You-Have-What-It-Takes.com** to download preliminary information, then E-Mail Julia if you think it's for you.

Other Books By Julia Hastings

Julia Hastings specialises in teaching mental picturing. Her books have been translated into several foreign languages.

Book - You Can Have What You Want, beautifully designed with 10 full paged cartoons shows you how to succeed in relationships, money and health. "You don't have to settle for second best, you can have what you want." This book will show you how. $12.95

Book - You're Great!, *Three Steps To Self-Confidence*
Self confidence comes from one thing: doing your
'This is it!' the activity that will bring you deep
happiness. Beautifully designed with many full paged
cartoons and a chapter on self-confidence and sex
appeal, this book will give you unshakeable self-
confidence that no one can take away. $12.95

Book - The Day Dream Diet, *The Inner Game Of
Dieting* is a truly inspiring book. Rejuvenate, shape-up
and create the future you want through mental
picturing. This book will help you succeed on any diet
of your choice, and, get the upper hand on eating
disorders. It's 'Silver Bullets' diet and beauty secrets
work like *magic.* You'll recognise the 'The Fat Monster'
and get him out of your life *forever.* $15.95

Special offers on books are listed on our Web Site
WWW.You-Have-What-It-Takes.com

You can do it!